Wagtail Flies Away

Learn About Migration

Mathangi Subramanian

Illustrated by Suvidha Mistry

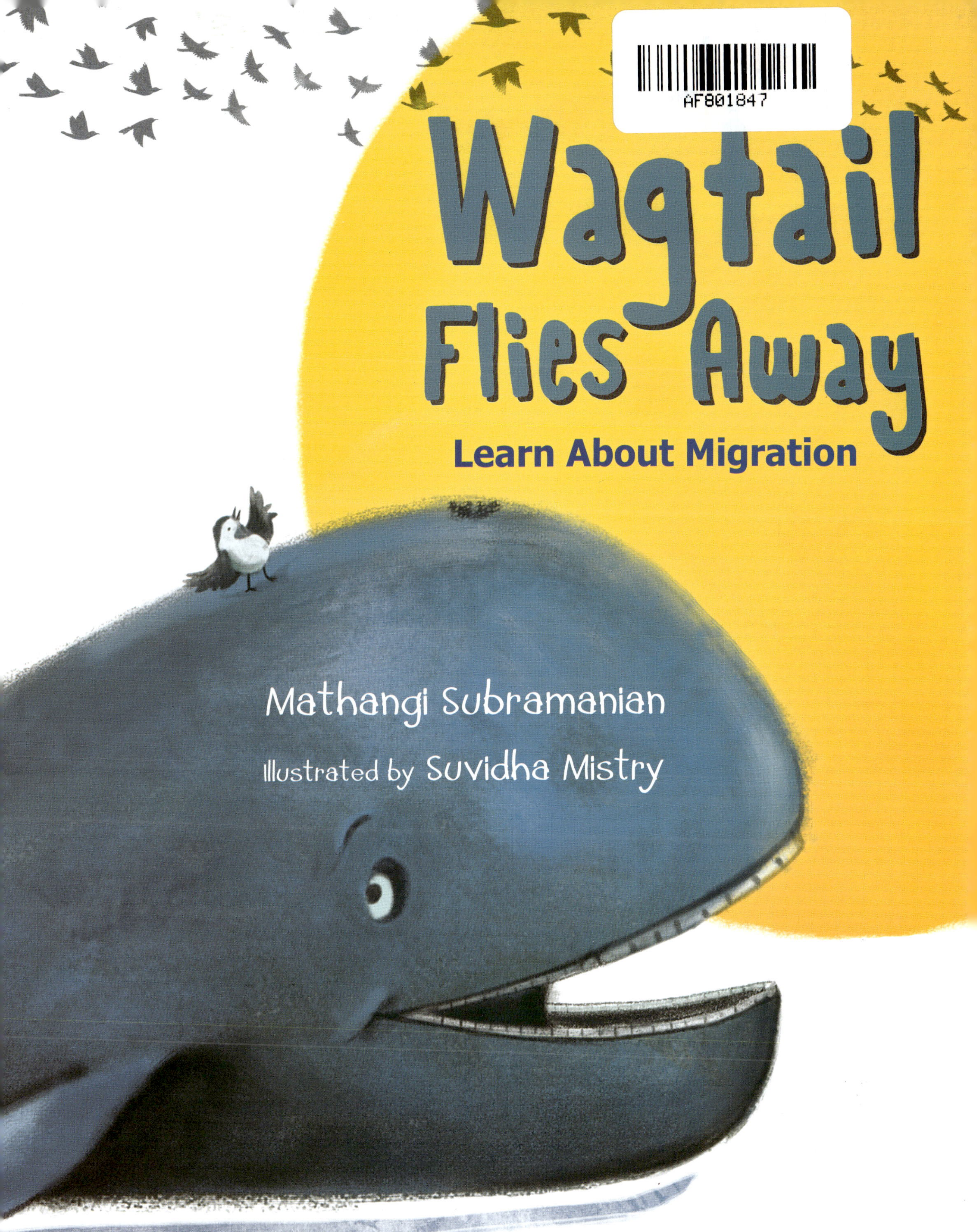

SCHOLASTIC
New York Toronto London Auckland
Sydney New Delhi Hong Kong

For

Prema Narasimhan

Mathangi Subramanian is the award-winning author of four books for children and young adults. Her shorter work has appeared in lots of places, including *The Hindu*, *The Indian Express*, *Kahani* and *Thinkling*. A former science teacher, she loves writing and learning about animals, birds and nature.

Suvidha Mistry is a freelance illustrator with a passion for all forms of art. She loves to tell stories with her illustrations, sketches and photography. She has worked with multimedia firms as a graphic head and now she is living her dream as an illustrator for children's books.

Published by Scholastic India Pvt. Ltd.
A subsidiary of Scholastic Inc., New York, 10012 (USA).
Publishers since 1920, with international operations in Canada, Australia, New Zealand, the United Kingdom, India, and Hong Kong.

For information regarding permission, write to:
Scholastic India Pvt. Ltd.
A-27, Ground Floor, Sigma Centre
Infocity-1, Sector 34, Gurgaon 122001 (India)

First edition: December 2016
This reprint edition : March 2026

ISBN-13: 978-93-8631-356-0

Printed in India at Sai Printo Pack Pvt. Ltd.

A NOTE ABOUT MIGRATION

Many animals and birds *migrate* twice a year. This means they travel long distances between the same places, usually to find food, start families or avoid very cold or very hot weather.

Migration is dangerous and difficult. During migration, birds may not eat for days. Animals may have to cross cities full of pollution and traffic. Insects that are just a few centimetres long may have to fly for hundreds of miles. Yet, every year, these amazing creatures successfully journey through the land, water and sky.

As humans, there are many things we can do to help our travelling friends. We can put out clean water and bird food in our yards, windowsills and balconies. We can plant native trees and plants. We can participate in beach clean-ups and stop throwing trash in local parks and waterways. Most importantly, we can teach our friends and family about respecting birds, animals and insects and the land that they depend on when they migrate.

Wagtail and Mama sat on the banks of the river.
The sun faded from the sky.

"The air is getting colder," Wagtail shivered.

"And the days are getting shorter," Mama said.
"It's time for us to go."

Scientists believe birds know they have to migrate when they notice the days getting shorter and the air getting colder.

"Go where?" Wagtail asked.

"The same place we go every year," Mama said. "Somewhere warm and sunny where we can find lots of delicious food."

"How far are we flying, Mama?" Wagtail asked.

"Across the ocean and then across the land" Mama said.

Birds prepare for migration by eating fatty, nutritious foods for months before the journey.

"What if I am not strong enough to fly so far?" Wagtail asked.

"You have been eating healthy food and growing strong for months," Mama said. "You are ready for this journey. Now get some rest. You will need it."

The next morning, the sky was crowded with wagtails.

"It's time," Mama said.

"How do we know the way?" Wagtail asked.

"We can tell from the way the sun is shining," Mama said. "We will smell the air for clues, too. And we will look for familiar places."

Wagtail and Mama swooped up into the sky.

Scientists think migrating birds navigate using the angle of the sun. They may also recognise smells like pine forests or pollution from cities, and remember landmarks from past journeys.

The flock flew over forests and plains and grasslands. Wagtail felt tired.

"You are tired because you are in the front of the flock," Mama said. "Try flying inside."

Wagtail moved into the middle of the group. The air did not sting her face. She did not have to fight the wind.

"In our flock, we all help each other," Mama said. "After you feel better, make sure you go to the front again, so that another bird can rest just like you have."

After many days, the flock came to the ocean.
The water made a gentle licking sound.

But what was that other sound?

Suddenly, the biggest animal Wagtail had ever seen rose out of the water. It was singing a beautiful melody.

"Are you migrating too?" Wagtail asked.

"Yes," said the creature. "I'm a humpback whale. I'm on my way to warmer waters, where I can find more food and escape the cold. Whenever I am on a long journey, I like to sing to pass the time."

"Will you teach me your song?" asked Wagtail.

"Of course," said the whale.

For many miles, whale's music filled the air.

The ocean stretched on and on. Wagtail had never seen so much water.

When they finally landed, Wagtail said, "It's one thing to migrate when you are the size of a whale. But how can a little bird like me fly so far?"

Just then, Wagtail saw a tiny, fuzzy insect.

"I'm a moth," it said. "I'm travelling many miles to lay eggs and start a family in a warm place."

"But you are so small!" Wagtail said. "Don't you get tired?"

"I use the wind," the moth said. "See?"

Some moths and butterflies migrate hundreds of kilometres by riding strong winds. Like birds, moths and butterflies also navigate using sunlight and landmarks. Some moths and butterflies even follow roads built by humans.

The moth spread her wings, leapt into a strong gust of wind and floated away. Wagtail tried too. She felt the air carry her. She didn't even have to flap her wings!

"I guess if this little moth can fly so far, then I can too," Wagtail thought.

After a huge meal and a long rest, Wagtail and the flock took to the skies. When they flew over mountains, Wagtail saw a group of animals almost as big as Whale.

"Who are you?" Wagtail asked.

"I 'm an elephant," the creature said. "Every year, my sisters, my children and I migrate when it rains. We've taken this path many times."

Asian elephants migrate in groups headed by the oldest female in the pack. Some elephants live for 60 years, and so make the same journey 60 times.

"How many?" Wagtail asked.

"More than thirty," Elephant said. "But my mother has done it twice as many times. That's why she is leading us."

Wagtail thought about taking the same journey 60 times. Now that would be something, she thought.

Wagtail and the flock flew over roads and farms and cities. After a while, she was tired again.

"Mama," Wagtail asked, "will we rest soon?"

"We used to rest here," Mama said. "But now, people have built their cities in our favourite places. See the train station? That used to be a lake."

Wagtail looked down. The earth was covered in buildings and roads and cars. At the train station, humans flowed in and out of rattling trains, carrying suitcases. Just like Wagtail, they were travelling far from their homes.

There was no place for a bird to rest.

Many human families migrate to cities in search of better jobs and education.

Finally, Wagtail and Mama landed on the banks of another river. "Welcome to our new home," Mama said. "How do you like it?"

The river gurgled and giggled. The sun was warm and gentle. The water was full of delicious insects.

Wagtail felt warm and cozy and safe.

"It's perfect!" she said.

Wagtail looked up and saw the flock fly away.

"We will meet them again when it is time to return," Mama said. "Now, let's eat and rest and grow strong again."

You can help migrating birds and animals by putting out food and water, planting native plants and trees and keeping wild areas litter-free.

Wagtail thought about all the creatures she had met who travelled by air, land and sea.

She thought about flying over oceans, cities, forests and plains.

She thought about singing songs with a whale, riding the wind with a moth and chatting with a family of elephants.

Mama said, "Do you like it here, little one?"

"I like it here," Wagtail said, "but what I really like is flying away!"

QUESTIONS FOR TEACHERS AND STUDENTS:

- Why do birds, animals and insects migrate?
- How do birds and animals know when to migrate?
- How do birds, animals and insects know where to go? In other words, how do they navigate?
- What are some challenges birds and animals face when they migrate?
- How do birds, animals and insects cope with the challenges they face during migration?
- Why do humans migrate?
- Have you and your family ever migrated? Do you know anyone who has migrated?
- What can we do to help migrating creatures?

ACTIVITIES FOR STUDENTS

- PLANT A MIGRATION GARDEN. Plant native plants, put out water, and hang bird feeders to give birds a place to rest when they migrate.
- WRITE YOUR OWN MIGRATION STORY. Interview a family member who has migrated. Who did they meet on their journey? How did they travel? What did they see? Write your own illustrated book about a family member's migration story.
- WRITE A WELCOME LETTER. What kinds of landmarks would a bird or an animal want to see if they were migrating through your area? Write a letter or draw a map of the parts of your home that you think a migrating animal or bird would like to see.
- DRAW A MIGRATION MAP. What animals or birds migrate through your area? Draw a map of the migration routes that different birds and animals take. Do the routes in different colours. What similarities do you see? What differences do you see?